The Brave Entrepreneur's Desk

121 Affirmations & Epiphanies for Motivation and Profits

Maria James

Empower Wealth Publishing

For permissions contact:
Pocket of Money, LLC info@pocketofmoney.com

For information about special discounts available for bulk purchases, sales promotions, fund-raising and educational needs, contact the author Maria James at 443-304-8896 or info@pocketofmoney.com. Website: www.pocketofmoney.com

Published by Empower Wealth Publishing.

ISBN: 978-1-7351805-0-2

Acknowledgements

I want to express my deepest gratitude and love for all the people who believe in me, my vision, and support my mission to financially empower others.

My parents taught me that I could do anything and have always supported my goals. They continuously push me to do and be better.

Thank you.

iv

BONUS:
Let's Network

Thank you for buying my book. I would like to offer you a free ticket to one of my virtual un-networking events.

These events will give you structured activities and time to showcase your expertise.

To claim your free ticket to the virtual un-networking event: https://pocketofmoney.com/bravegift

Traditional networking events are usually inefficient, ineffective, and a bit tedious. Online, it's a similar process.

Let's evolve this process. We have a much better way to showcase yourself, learn about others, and establish mutually beneficial relationships.

Table of Contents

Chapter 1: Entrepreneurship is Complex

Entrepreneurship. It can take you to such highs and yet can also drive you crazy.

You'll hear numerous people discuss the benefits and extoll the virtues of entrepreneurship, which are all valid. It's amazing when you can create your own schedule. It is great to be able to work on something every day that excites you.

Creating a money earning machine that has an almost unlimited capacity for you to gain financial freedom is amazing. The fact that you can gain financial freedom to create time freedom allowing you to focus on activities and people that you love is incredible.

However, entrepreneurship is not all sunshine, rainbows, and complete autonomy. Just as there are fabulous benefits, there are also some really hard conditions and truths about the entrepreneurship journey.

The struggle of making a name for yourself within your market, worrying if the sales are sufficient to pay bills, and thrive while wearing all or many of the hats in your business is stressful. There are innumerable other struggles and worries, but you get the point. As an entrepreneur, you know them well.

I have a major issue with the advice and conversations about entrepreneurship. There is too much discussion of the benefits and not enough information or talk about the hard times, and most importantly what it takes to make it through those hard times.

Saying that the entrepreneur journey is tough is a MAJOR understatement. It tests you in so many ways. When people say that this journey is not for everyone, this is the unabashed truth. I, for one, have the "scars" to prove it.

After earning my doctorate, I jumped feet first, into entrepreneurship. I had a plan, albeit (in hindsight) not a great one. However, using the knowledge and experience that I had, I created the best strategy that I could.

While looking for jobs, I did research and read books and blog articles, on starting up a for-profit business. Once I felt I had a good enough grasp on it, I wrote a step-by-step strategy based on my research. I then got to work implementing it. Within 30 days, I created my first product which explained how to accelerate saving money and save consistently. I then created a website to sell my product.

My product was a kit that detailed a six-factor system. It included a guide, an audio lesson, the audio lesson script, and money management templates for budgeting and tracking spending. I thought it was awesome. After getting three people to test it I received a lot of feedback. Constructive criticism is always a good thing.

After having six manuscripts torn apart before publication in peer-reviewed journals during graduate school, I knew the importance of not taking criticism personally and implementing the feedback. I had to be okay with the fact that what I thought was good was not ready to be sold just yet. After revising each item based on the feedback, I thought, "okay now I'm good to go, I just have to let people know about it".

We all know the power of social media and its continuous growth. It is possible to gain millions of followers who pay attention to what you post or have to say. Individuals with a large number of followers on a social media platform are called influencers. The term influencer was officially added to the dictionary in 2019. That in itself lets you know how pervasive social media and influencers are in daily life and our businesses.

As an entrepreneur, you've seen the advice: create a personal brand on social platforms, grow your following, and occasionally post information about what your business offers. Many are led to believe that this is all they have to do and then BOOM; sales will come pouring into the business.

Well, that is not quite the way it goes. When I started my for-profit business in 2013, social media was already quite powerful. Although at that time I wasn't yet familiar with the term influencer. I figured with a few social media posts and my website I could let people know that I had this amazing product for sale and people would buy.

I thought, of course, everyone would be able to see that my product is amazing. I couldn't imagine anyone who didn't want to get help saving more money. I truly believed I was ready to send my product out into the world to help others, and now I would have a successful business.

I had earned a PhD from one of the most prestigious universities in the nation, surely this couldn't be that much harder. I also co-founded and helped run a non-profit for ten years. As I wasn't starting completely from scratch, and I'd done the research, I knew what I needed to be successful. I had convinced myself that I'd made a good strategy for this business and I would now make it work.

So naïve! Yes, I know. However, I didn't know that at the time.

My time and energy started to shift from searching for jobs to working hard in my business. Being self-employed was so much more attractive than working for someone else, and the idea of an uncapped income was especially attractive. I knew it would be a lot of work but figured I could do it.

I made less than seventy-five dollars and lived on my savings for eight months. At this stage, I had to admit that I did not know what I was doing. It was extremely difficult to watch my savings dwindle while earning no revenue.

A few times a week, I would analyze my budget trying to determine what else I could cut. I'm extremely frugal, but I got to the point where there was nothing more to cut from my budget.

I wasn't making it work. I did not have the knowledge or the experience to figure out exactly what wasn't working and why. What I did realize and accept was that I could not do this alone. Without help, I would run myself and my fledgling business into the ground. I had to get help, then and there before I didn't have the resources to do it.

My saving grace was hiring a business coach who pointed out the countless mistakes I was making. Whew, I realized that there was so much to running and marketing an online for-profit business that I did not know. With coaching, I figured out my target audience and revised my revenue streams.

I had to overhaul my entire business model. This entailed creating both a marketing strategy and sales funnel. Both of which were completely missing before getting coaching. With these modifications, I went from making $73.47 in twelve months to almost $1,400 in thirty days.

The major point of this story is that it took me a year to see that change. A full year of mistakes, coaching, learning, and implementing. If I wasn't able to keep myself motivated and maintain the passion during those twelve months, then I would have quit and never seen the results.

I could have been a statistic, one of the many businesses that fail within their first year. If I had not been honest with myself and hired a coach, I definitely would have failed. There is nothing wrong and everything right with realizing you need help. Get it from those who have been there and made mistakes that they can teach you to avoid.

The entrepreneurship journey is full of ups and downs and being strong enough not to give up during the down times. Failure is only temporary if you keep working and don't give up. This will ensure that a situation that didn't work out will move from a failure to a failure moment. You have to continue on the journey, to reach success, and reap the tantalizing benefits that drew you into entrepreneurship in the first place.

Progressing through any failure is usually much easier said than done. One thing that helped me through that first year and still helps me through any failure moment today is the use of affirmations.

I used to be ambivalent about affirmations, only because I didn't realize I use them. I always considered it pumping myself up and logically working through a situation or scenario.

I am generally great at motivating and re-motivating myself when necessary. However, even I find it difficult to bounce back during some failure moments. This is when I started writing down motivational statements that I could read when I was doubting myself or trying to bounce back after a failure moment.

In the upcoming chapters, I'm going to share lessons that I learned about the most common misconceptions regarding entrepreneurship and failure. This includes specific "advice" that is just wrong, but we've all heard and probably tried to follow.

I also simply messed up a lot and want to share so that you don't have to make the same mistakes. This truth will allow you to avoid these mistakes that could potentially cost you thousands of dollars.

I will also share affirmations that I use to stay motivated. These help me to refocus, especially after experiencing failure, having to work through a hard struggle, or overcome a tough obstacle.

Chapter 2: The Financial Journey

If you are already in business, then you understand the importance of cash flow. Irrespective of whether you started your business out of a strong desire to help people, create multiple income streams, increase your household income, or you wanted to be your own boss, you know a business has to make money.

Cash flow is a non-negotiable necessity for any successful and healthy business. Hmm, let me be more specific. **<u>Positive</u>** cash flow is a necessity for any successful and healthy business. You cannot function without revenue coming into your business that can be used to pay operational expenses such as inventory, marketing and advertising, and business development. A negative cash flow is a major red flag and a sign of a business in trouble.

When you start studying entrepreneurship and business, you will see phrases like "six-figure income" or "six-figure business" thrown around a lot. They are used everywhere. Many experts will advertise or flaunt making six figures and living the laptop lifestyle.

The laptop lifestyle refers to being able to work from any geographic location while earning money online. The term six-figures is thrown around so much that it is often included in revenue goals. I've seen that as the first revenue goal for several aspiring and recent entrepreneurs.

There is nothing wrong with aiming to earn six figures in a month or a year. However, if you're just getting started or your current revenue is nowhere near that amount, then it is advisable that you stairstep your revenue goals to reach this six-figure amount. In other words, you will need to include realistic incremental revenue goals.

Let's go through the entrepreneurship financial journey phases so you can better understand how to set your primary and intermediate revenue goals. No matter where you are on this journey, setting intermediate or incremental revenue goals will help you maintain your progress and motivation.

The entrepreneurship journey can correlate with and is marked by the financial phases and growth of your business. There are seven phases of the entrepreneur financial journey.

- Phase 1 – Startup
- Phase 2 – Profitless
- Phase 3 – Balance
- Phase 4 – Advancement
- Phase 5 – Freedom Bound
- Phase 6 – Expansion
- Phase 7 – Elevation

You are going to go through all of these phases. For your business to be successful, you have to earn enough revenue and profit to progress through these phases. To reach your definition of success, you will have to bring in the level of revenue that will allow you to pay yourself what you desire.

It is not always just about money. Your journey is also to fulfill your "why". What was the reason you started your business in the first place? What did you want the money to allow you to do? These are personal goals and a lifestyle that you want. You know your business can help you achieve them. Okay, let's break down and explain what's happening in each phase.

The 7 Financial Phases

Phase 1: Startup

The first phase is the startup phase. Here you are in planning and development mode. Having determined your business idea and niche, a lot of time is spent designing your business model and doing market and industry research. You're figuring out which revenue streams apply to your business.

You have started one or at least picked the first revenue stream that you're going to implement. Once that is complete, figure out marketing, distribution, and fulfillment (how you're getting the product or service to the customer). Your startup expenses have been calculated and you're purchasing all necessary equipment, software, domains, etc. These are one-time expenses that are required to operate and get your business off the ground.

Therefore, you're putting money into your business while no revenue is being earned. If you're bootstrapping the business funding, then you're using some personal money likely from your paycheck or savings. Perhaps you have received some outside help in the form of small investors, grants, or loans to fund your business startup.

To recap, in phase one, there is no revenue being earned, the cash flow is negative and you're likely still doing a lot of planning and research. However, you are implementing the plan and have started your business.

Phase 2: Profitless

Preliminary planning is complete. You have maintained the gains from phase one. Your products or services have been clearly defined. Your offer is clear and attractive to potential customers and/or clients. You have started to build up an audience. Some sales are now happening.

You have some revenue coming into your business and each revenue stream has a 30% gross profit margin or at least the industry standard. However, the amount of revenue still has not surpassed your expenses. You are not yet making a profit. Your cash flow is still negative.

Since your cash flow is still negative, you need to increase revenue to achieve good financial standing, especially as you're still using personal money to help fund your business and cover operational expenses.

Phase 3: Balance

In this phase, you have increased your sales and are earning a lot more revenue. You have established at least one consistent revenue stream. The key word here being "consistent". Your monthly revenue is enough to cover operational expenses and the cost of goods sold.

The cost of goods sold is the expenses directly related to a specific product or service. Your business as a whole is not yet making a profit, but it's no longer losing money. The money coming in is the same amount as the money going out.

In other words, the total revenue earned is equal to the total expenses paid. Your monthly revenue has surpassed the revenue you earned in phase two, and has been maintained for several months, ideally a year. I say ideally a year since many businesses will notice an ebb and flow in their revenue throughout twelve-months. You should be able to determine whether this surge or drop was due to a specific reason, such as a holiday season.

Most entrepreneurs are relieved when they reach this stage as it solidifies the "I can do this" feeling. You know if you can make it to the breakeven stage then you can surpass it. If you keep doing the work, working smarter, and failing forward, then you will keep increasing the profitability of your business.

Phase 4: Advancement
In phase four, you're finally making a profit. Your total revenue earned is consistently surpassing the total expenses. You've determined which systems are working well for your business and you're optimizing these to increase revenue and profitability.

Your goal is to further increase awareness about your business and what you offer. Your focus is on showcasing how you can help people so that you can increase sales and can grow your profits. People cannot buy from a business they don't know exists They won't buy from a business if they don't know that it offers what they need or want.

You have also continued to maintain a business gross profit margin of at least 30% and have had no zero revenue months. I know too well the pain of those types of months with no money coming into the business. Instead, you have a predictable positive cash flow and you're decreasing your liabilities.

Phase 5: Freedom Bound

In phase five, you have multiple revenue streams after having added one or two additional. You now have a business that is making enough of a profit to provide your desired salary, run your household, take care of the business operations, and still have money left over.

You have a good profit margin for the business as a whole as well as for each revenue stream. You're gaining financial freedom and the ability to live the lifestyle you desired. By now you have maintained a gross profit margin of 30% or surpassed it. You have established an engaged client and/or customer base with consistent revenue coming in from multiple revenue streams.

Most entrepreneurs are excited to reach this stage. You feel as though your dream or vision is finally turning into a reality. Not only is the business thriving, but you're now able to put more money towards personal financial goals. Achieving your desired financial freedom and living your desired lifestyle is all becoming a reality.

Phase 6: Expansion

Phase six is about growth. You start working on expanding to at least six to eight revenue streams. Keep in mind that expansion is likely to cause growth in expenses. Additional staff, more business systems, and advancing current business systems will be required to handle your growing customer base.

Designing the order of implementation of additional revenue streams has to be carefully structured, as you can't add several at once. Prioritize the order in which you will implement these new revenue streams based on your financial data and market research.

Upgrade business systems and hire contractors or employees to ensure that you will be able to handle the additional sales. Always maintain a positive and awesome experience for your clients and/or customers.

You are still maintaining a gross profit margin of 30% or more. Your loyal client and/or customer base that you've been nurturing gives your business predictable revenue and profits. In this phase, your current cash level (money in the bank - not revenue) and assets more than cover your current liabilities.

Phase 7: Elevation and Transition

The last phase of the entrepreneur finance journey is elevation and transition. Every entrepreneur is building their business for a different reason and end goal.

You may be building your business to sell it for a large sum of money. Or your goal may be to create a legacy and you will transfer ownership to someone in your household, generally a relative. That is the final phase: transfer ownership or sell it for a profit.

Surviving to Profitability

For many new entrepreneurs, the number one struggle is cash flow. Trying to earn the positive cash flow necessary to progress through these phases is tough and many in phases one through three do not have a lot of cash on hand. Those who fail during these phases usually had insufficient startup funding and were not growing their revenue fast enough to survive until profitability.

It is vital to have proper funding to be able to run your household and operate your business until the business profitable. The profit then has to be enough to sustain the business and your household in order to survive. Even with the best idea in the world, if you cannot survive to profitability, then you are setting yourself up to fail.

Making it through phases one to three is the toughest part of this journey. It is the trials and failures during these phases that will determine who will become a successful entrepreneur and who will give up.

Given that you have a sound business plan and a large enough market for what you offer, you still need to have enough money set aside to ensure survival until profitability. You may have to be able to sustain this for a couple of years. A large market and a sound plan do not automatically shorten phases one through three.

You have to be able to survive until you earn consistent revenue and a sufficient profit. Notice that I said profit and not until you start earning revenue. Remember in the beginning, you'll be earning revenue, but it will not be enough to cover expenses allowing your business to earn a profit.

Follow the four steps below to increase the likelihood of you surviving through any low revenue periods or large and unexpected expenses.

1) Create a personal finance plan.

You need to create what I call a bare-bones budget. This should only include items that are absolutely necessary for you and your family to survive. Determine your survival number.

The **survival number** is the amount of money needed to run your household, just to pay all your bills and eat. This budget will not only be necessary to start as a full-time entrepreneur but will also get you through tough times.

Remember to add items such as health, dental, and life insurance. As you'll be paying for these, I suggest you shop around for good rates.

2) Create a personal emergency fund.

With your survival number in mind, plan how much money you need to set aside to ensure that you're able to keep your home running sufficiently until profitability.

Your business plan should contain the hypothesis (an educated guess) as to when you will achieve profitability. As you work on building your business, you won't have to agonize about paying your household bills and staying alive.

3) Create a business financial plan.
As you should have a business budget, create a bare-bones budget for your business too. Determine your **operations number**. This is the amount of money necessary to run your business monthly. Anticipate how this number may change as you work on increasing revenue to the point of sustainability and then profitability.

4) Create an operations fund.
Your operations number determines how much money you need to reserve for the business. This amount should be set aside to operate your business until you reach profitability. You can then continue the core functions of your business while working on getting your business established in the market and achieving consistent revenue streams.

The total value of your survival number plus your operations number should be set aside to cover at least 18 months of expenses, as it is likely to take you that long to establish a consistent revenue stream and be consistently profitable. As you build your business make sure that the model is scalable. This is vital to be able to scale the business to continue increasing revenue.

To move past phase three, you need:
- An emergency fund for the household
- A reserve of operations capital for your business
- A scalable business model
- A financial system that can handle business growth
- Products and services that are priced for success
- A sales funnel that converts

Your entrepreneur financial journey will be powerful. It will be the most fun and the most stress you will ever have, but it won't be traveled overnight. The length of the journey depends on you, your planning, your financial acumen, your dedication, and your passion. To continue progressing and to accelerate this progression on your financial journey, you must:
- Acquire business resources and knowledge
- Acquire industry knowledge
- Establish a relationship with your customers/clients
- Fail forward

Have a strong financial plan and meet certain financial and business milestones before taking the leap into full-time entrepreneurship and you will be more likely to succeed. If you're already a full-time entrepreneur, work on setting those cash reserves aside.

The Journey is Not Timed
There is no time cap on each phase. A business can be operating for five months or five years and still be in the startup phase. Each phase can last for months or years,

which is why there are specific milestones listed for each phase.

Don't judge your entrepreneur journey by the stories of other entrepreneurs. You don't have the same resources, time schedule, responsibilities, or mentors. You'll move through the phases faster than some but slower than others. As long as you stay motivated and keep moving, you will continue reaching new levels of success.

Chapter 3: Your Why Is Important

It can be extremely frustrating when nothing seems to be going right. Sometimes you just want to throw your hands up and yell "can one thing go right, please!" Actually, I'm pretty sure I've done that before ... many times. I've also taken a deep breath, closed the computer very slowly, and just walked away because I was getting too frustrated and angry. At such times, when the self-doubt springs up and you feel overwhelmed, you start to question: "Can I do this? What am I doing wrong? Should I let this go?"

Several years ago, I had a really tough time, having just started financial consulting. I had just finished working with two clients and felt great. I really felt, "okay, I can do this." I had three potential clients lined up which after about two months of back-and-forth emails and calls were each at the proposal stage. All had settled on the length of the consulting agreement, their start dates, and each had received their individual tailored proposals. All that was left to do was to review and sign the proposals.

In what felt like one day, all three potential clients informed me that they had decided not to start my consulting program. While each person's actual wording or reason was different, the result was the same. They were not signing up and there was no more objection handling that could be done. I went from having wrapped up two successful happy clients and being ready to start with three new clients to having no clients and an empty client queue.

My revenue had dried up. My level of frustration and melancholy was extremely high. A bit of anxiety joined this pity party and before long the not so good companion, self-doubt, raised its head and joined too.

Self-doubt is like an annoying fly buzzing around. The buzzing drives you crazy, then suddenly you don't hear it anymore and you think it's gone. You feel it's safe to start eating your favorite meal. Just as you are in full swing enjoying your meal you hear the buzzing again and the fly zooms past your face. It was never gone. It was merely looking for an opportunity to pop up again.

A tough situation and the arising self-doubt that follows can negatively affect your productivity. It can be difficult to focus. You find yourself being inconsistent as that high energy burn and passion to utilize every minute that you can to work on your business starts to wane.

This is when the self-doubt goes up a level and the second round of questions begin. It is said "if it's your passion then it won't feel like work." You start to question; "This really feels like a lot of work. Is this not my passion? Is this not my purpose? Should I be doing something else? Should I let this entrepreneur thing go?"

In moments like this, the first thing you should do is to pause and take a step back. Literally walk away from the computer, the office, the co-working space, whatever space you use to do your work for your business. Once you have removed yourself from your workspace, BREATHE.

Take several calming breaths which does work to help you refocus and re-center yourself. After taking several breaths, engage in a de-stress activity. This does not have to be something expensive or anything elaborate. De-stress activities are different for all of us. It can be reading a book, watching a video, watching a movie, cleaning, ironing, going for a walk or run, quality time with loved ones or playing with a pet. Do whatever works for you.

Pick an activity that allows you to regain your positivity and decrease the levels of overwhelm, anxiety, and stress. I suggest finding a free or low-cost activity.

If you are in financial phases one through three, then money is still pretty tight. As you don't have much or any extra discretionary income, a free activity won't cause you additional stress or guilt from spending even more money, that is not going towards your business.

My de-stress activities are going for a walk, reading a fictional book, watching movies, and hanging out with family. There's nothing like a family movie night to help me de-stress and not think about business.

Step four is to revisit your why. Why did you start your business? Why is it so important that you succeed?

Don't say to make money. Money is just a tool. It's always more than that, so making money is not your why. Your why is about what you want the money to be able to do. Revisit the real reason you want to make money. I've heard many "whys" over the years.

- I want enough money to go on vacation every quarter.
- I want to pay for my children's college education so that they don't need to be burdened with student loans.
- I want to show my children that it is possible and to be an example.

- I want to live my best life and I need money to get the things I want and do what I want.
- I want to be my own boss forever.

Whatever your reason is for starting a business and wanting to be successful is fine. Revisit this reason and remember its importance to help you weather these frustrating times. This will remind you why you have to succeed and help rekindle that fire to make your dream a reality.

Once you have lowered your stress level, it's time to get re-motivated. There will always be times where you have to re-motivate yourself. That initial spark of motivation is not enough to see you through the completion of your goals. Have some tricks you can use to pump yourself up.

I strongly recommend affirmations and reviewing your goals. This works wonders for me. Repeating the affirmations will help to get you into the right mindset and pump you up to get back to work. Reviewing your goals will remind you of what you are aiming to accomplish and get you even more pumped.

Just because it feels like work does NOT mean this business is not your passion or purpose. Running a business is WORK. Being an entrepreneur is a lot of work.

There will be days when the tasks needed to move your projects and business forward will feel tough and others when the hours just fly by and you're really enjoying the tasks. Neither type of day qualifies or disqualifies you as a real and passionate entrepreneur.

If you have more days where it's a real struggle than days when it's not, it still does not mean this is not your passion. What it does mean is that something in your business is broken and desperately needs to be fixed. You will need to analyze your:

- business model
- revenue streams
- sales funnel
- target audience
- manufacturing/creation process
- distribution
- marketing
- automation

You should automate as much of your business systems and processes as possible. This will allow you to focus more time and energy on revenue-generating activities while decreasing the stress of managing so many moving parts.

Automation is also crucial to being able to scale. You cannot do the majority of tasks in real-time in your business. Many of the tasks should be automated or accomplished with software. Your customer-facing tasks should not be automated, as personalization and caring goes a long way.

To recap, when you feel overwhelmed, this is the reset protocol:
1. Take a step back.
2. Breathe.
3. Do a de-stress activity.
4. Revisit your why.
5. Re-motivate.

Chapter 4: Go Hard or Go Home

Go hard or go home. As an entrepreneur, you hear this repeated constantly. After hearing this (or an equivalent phrase) so often as an aspiring or recent entrepreneur, you adopt it as your mantra thinking it's the entrepreneurship way. You think to be a "real" entrepreneur you have to exhibit this characteristic and adhere closely to this rule.

I thought I knew what this phrase meant: give your business your all, work hard to pursue and actualize your dreams, turn your dreams into reality; don't be timid, and really push for it. On the surface this seems like great work ethic. Put in the work to achieve your goals.

Sounds great right? Unfortunately, the way the implementation of this rule shows up is for entrepreneurs (to an extent) to ignore family, friends, and non-business events for a while. You are encouraged by others to put your nose to the grindstone while forgoing these relationships and activities to achieve your goals. While this is doable for a short time, over a long period it can lead to burnout and damaged relationships.

Business success a.k.a. moving through the financial phases takes years. Yes, as I mentioned, everyone has a different story. Some will move through the different phases faster than others. However, if you sit and speak to successful entrepreneurs, you will find that no one is an overnight success.

NO ONE is an overnight success. To achieve the level of business and financial success that makes you want to study them usually takes years of work, consistent work.

You can't ignore relationships and life while working on your business. You can only keep your nose to the grindstone for short periods and then you need to look up, take a breath, and find enjoyment in the journey. It will do you no good to reach success, whatever that looks and feels like for you, only to have destroyed your relationships and let life pass you by.

Go hard or go home does not mean working yourself into the ground. I learned this the hard way. You're probably used to working hard in your business as you know it's instrumental to your success. Can you imagine not being able to work in or on your business at all?

Yeah ... I went through that due to implementing "go hard or go home" the wrong way. I want to share some things that I learned.

Business Lessons – A Cautionary Tale

I couldn't use my hands! No seriously, I could NOT use my hands. Therefore, I couldn't work on my business at all. This led to some epiphanies and reiterated some previously learned lessons. I'm going to share with you, both what happened to my hands and those business and personal finance lessons.

I'd had issues with my hand before, so I should have realized what I was doing to myself, but at the time I was just too excited and focused on my new project. I was building out a new platform, contacting vendors, creating, testing, optimizing, and of course this was on top of my regular business duties.

You know when you have a really exciting new idea or new project for your business, you tend to become slightly obsessed? I

25

would make a cup of tea and sit at my computer typing and clicking away.

You're pumped about every bit of progress that you make so you can't wait to work on it every day. You do some market testing of your idea and get a ton of positive feedback.

Yeah that was me. Without realizing it I had become obsessed, spending way too much time constantly working at my computer without taking any breaks. Being totally engrossed with business tasks, the HOURS would fly by.

Next thing I knew, I started feeling pain in both hands (carpal and metacarpal areas).

I did listen to my body and started taking a few breaks. I bought wrist braces and a vertical mouse. I was already using a track ball mouse and figured maybe I needed to switch between that and a vertical one.

But despite these measures, it had reached the point where I could not work on my computer for longer than 20 minutes. After this time, I would be in such pain, looking at my hands and saying "seriously?!"

I developed tendonitis in both wrists.

I went to the doctor to see if that was really my diagnosis, and yes it was. Thankfully, I did not need surgery or any real medication, but the orders received from the doctor were "do not do any work effective IMMEDIATELY" ... in other words, sit down and rest, you workaholic!

If I did not heed the doctor's advice, then injections and possibly surgery would have been in my future. As I do not like needles (as a matter of fact I abhor them) and I did not want to get cut ... I stopped working.

As an entrepreneur, you know your business is like your baby, and suddenly I couldn't take care of my baby. I had been making such progress and then nothing, full steam ahead and then a crashing halt. The level of frustration I felt was pretty much indescribable.

I may have gone a little crazy, but can we say wake-up call!

While I was stressing and not able to do work, I had a lot of time to think and reflect. So, let's get to the business lessons. Learn from my mistakes so that you don't have to suffer the same situations and loss of revenue.

Business Lesson 1: Passive income is crucial.
You know you should have multiple revenue streams, but how many passive revenue streams do you have now and how many do you plan to add? I always tell entrepreneurs that they need to have passive income and earned income.

My tendonitis situation is the epitome to support this lesson. I now have more appreciation of the importance of passive income. With passive income, you do a lot of work upfront to create a quality solution, so your direct time and energy are no longer necessary to earn revenue.

Having passive income is great, for if you suddenly can't use something necessary to bring in revenue, such as your hands, your voice, your legs, or your whatever. During that time, you can still have money coming into the business. Now take it a step further and ask yourself "how much money would come into my business?"

How much of your total revenue is passive? Would it be enough to keep operations going and pay you if you're already self-employed?

If the answer is no, then you may want to fix the situation. How?

1) You should know your operations number and survival number. Remember we mentioned these in chapter two. Your operations number is the bare minimum dollar amount to run your business per month. Your survival number is the bare minimum dollar amount to run your household per month.

2) Design and optimize sales funnels for your passive revenue streams. Work at creating consistent revenue from your passive sources. Sales funnels are your tool to creating consistent sales, so don't be discouraged if you feel like "I'm trying!" and haven't gotten it down yet. It can take a while to optimize each sales funnel. Keep going.

3) Aim to get your sales funnels for your passive revenue streams to be at least equal to the total for your operations plus your survival number. It will be worth it. Imagine if your bare-bones numbers could be met with passive income? You would know the bills would always be covered.

Depending on your industry it may be very difficult or near impossible to increase your passive revenue to that amount. Get as close to it as you can.

Business Lesson 2: Have a plan to remove yourself from the business.

You may be thinking, "What?! I am the business! It's MY skills and knowledge that are offered, I keep things running."

Let me explain. You should be prepared to hand off the vast majority of tasks for your business and spend your time on tasks that ONLY you can do. Depending on where you are in business this may take quite a while, but understand that this should be a goal.

The more time that you spend on revenue-generating activities, and crafting or optimizing solutions, the more money you will make.

Write or record SOPs (standard operating procedures) for EVERYTHING. I wish that I had completed and followed through with this task. My list of tasks to delegate for every project had already been written, but ... I figured I had plenty of time before I would actually need the SOPs.

However, as it stood, even if I risked needles and scalpels, and struggled through the pain to use the computer to find a contractor, I didn't have anything to hand off. I hadn't written the procedures or protocols for important tasks. Only those given to contractors, already hired for specific tasks, had been recorded.

If you're the only person in your business or just starting and don't have staff or contractors, then you may well be doing everything for a while. Still make sure that these procedures are written out. When you can hire assistance, the onboarding will be faster and smoother.

Don't be the bottleneck of your business and your revenue.

1) Hire contractors or freelancers for tasks that you can delegate. With written or recorded SOPs, you can easily delegate any task. To eliminate almost all questions and potential misunderstandings, I found that follow along videos are excellent.

2) Use tools and resources that simplify tasks, thus reducing the time and energy needed. For example, scheduling social media takes up way too much time for me, so I invested in scheduling software and delegate this task to a virtual assistant. I write the content. The contractor creates images and uploads my words and these images to the social media scheduling software.

What tasks can you delegate in your business? By how much do you need to increase your revenue to hire assistance?

Business lesson 3: Grow up to it, not into it.
When I had to stop working my revenue was in free fall. While I could not use my hands, I kept thinking "how am I going to stop this free fall!?"

I put my finance cap on and took a hard look at the expenses in my business. I said to myself, "hmmm, now is the time to treat this like I would a personal finance budget."

I had to get real and ask myself some tough questions.

After analyzing my expenses, I realized some services were just not delivering the expected return on investment (ROI). Whether it was the service itself or my ability to use it didn't matter at that point.

I found alternative tools and software to do or replace the things I had let go and still allow me to serve in the same capacity. I was amazed that this was possible.

Now here's the kicker. I decreased my expenses by 67% and could still operate at full capacity, delivering services and products with the same experience for my clients and customers. I could now run my business with a third of the money I used before.

I realized that I used software that had functions and capabilities that my business was not yet ready to fully utilize, as well as using services with the expectation of growing into them. These functions were not crucial to my business function.

What really convinced me was taking a look at some mentors that make six figures a month that used services I thought were for budding entrepreneurs. I remember saying to myself, "if they don't need this software to make that kind of money neither do I."

Don't pay for a service with the hope and expectation that using it will increase your revenue or that your business will grow into it.

Instead, use services you can afford with your current revenue. Focus on growing your revenue to upgrade your business software and tools. It is possible to upgrade your business systems without upgrading the software or hiring expensive contractors.

Software is not synonymous with systems.

The SOPs we discussed in business lesson two will help you systematize your business. Consistently analyzing your financial data will help you determine when you can upgrade certain tools. Of course, this data can also be used to determine when you can add or launch additional revenue streams.

Personal Finance Lessons – A Cautionary Tale

There are a few personal finance concepts that are crucial. While some may be very simple; they are still crucial.

I want to reiterate some of those crucial financial lessons that bolster your financial security. I say reiterate because these are all concepts you've probably heard before. Let's talk about them because it's easy to set things aside and not realize their importance.

Personal Finance Lesson 1: An emergency fund is your airbag.

You may have heard that having an emergency fund is important. Well, it's not important… it is crucial. This is one of the tools that are vital to stay safe and survive a financial emergency.

With a sudden medical emergency, like my situation, comes unexpected expenses. Imagine if something like this happened to you. You may need to purchase medical prescriptions, braces for a limb, maybe have a procedure (or several procedures), purchase other medical equipment, and foot the bill for a host of expenses that you can't even think of yet.

With any type of emergency, it's very unlikely that you'll know what it will cost. That's the great thing about an emergency fund. It will help decrease your stress knowing that you already have the money to take care of these unexpected expenses. If they are going to cost more than you have in your emergency fund, you can at least handle some key expenses while you figure out what to do about the rest.

A medical emergency is a common unexpected expense. In the United States, the average medical emergency can cost anything from a couple of hundred dollars to a few thousand dollars. Even with insurance you will pay this amount.

Therefore, to start it is important to put aside an amount in this range of at least $2,500 into your emergency fund. Of course, putting in more is a much much much better idea. A complete emergency fund is six to nine months' worth of monthly expenses.

Aim for at least three months' worth of bills saved in your emergency fund. Use intermediate goals to reach your saving goal. Start with $500 as the very bare minimum. The second goal can be to reach $1,500, then aim for $2,500. Use as many intermediate goals as necessary until you achieve three months' worth of expenses saved.

I know that almost a year's worth of monthly expenses set aside is a lot of money and it may take quite a while to reach this goal. Keep adding money, every single month, into your emergency fund and you'll get there. Make sure your emergency fund is in a separate saving account from any other saving goals.

Add saving as a category in your budget. This should be in the fixed expenses section to make sure it gets paid every month. Treat it like a bill and make it the first bill that you pay. Consider calling that category something such as Financial Security instead of Saving. By naming it as the reason why you need (not should but need) to save can act as a great reminder as to why it's so important to make sure this savings bill gets paid.

There is a specific dollar amount that you can put into your emergency fund every month. I don't care what that dollar amount is. If this is literally 1 dollar, so what. Put that amount into your savings every month. As you continue to progress on your financial journey, you will be able to increase that dollar amount.

Personal Finance Lesson 2: Multiple streams of income are a must.

What would happen if you suddenly can't work? Or if you don't have enough money or paid leave from a job to be out of work long enough for your recovery? Where would you get the money to cover your bills?

This is when multiple income streams will be a lifesaver. The great thing about having income from more than one source is that if one income source becomes disrupted or stops, all of your income does NOT stop. In times where all income sources are flowing, you will have more money to put towards your financial goals.

The more money you put towards financial goals, the faster you'll reach them. For example, by increasing the amount going towards your emergency fund, the faster you will reach that goal.

Whether you're a full-time entrepreneur or an employed professional building your business on the side (a side hustle), you have to have multiple sources of income or revenue.

There is nothing wrong with starting your business as a side hustle. A side hustle used to simply be a second job working for someone else. You had your primary job, what people would call your 9 to 5, and your side hustle was then a second job working in the evenings or on weekends.

However, the rapid pace of technology and the increased acceptance of freelancers and contractors have turned a side hustle into something of your own creation. A side hustle can be the start of a new business or entrepreneurial venture that is completely reliant on you. Something where you use your skills and knowledge to offer solutions to people. You can and should exercise entrepreneurial tendencies.

If you're an aspiring entrepreneur, let me speak to that for just a moment.

You don't have to start a new business that you want to grow into an empire. You see that in so many places: "I'm working on my empire." or "I'm building an empire." You don't have to be working on the next Facebook or Google. You can use your skills and knowledge to bring in an extra few hundred or thousand dollars per month.

Your idea does not have to be something complex or some never seen before magical service or product. Not only is that incredibly hard to do, but it's also very RISKY. Start something where you already see people making money.

You may be thinking ... WHY? Doesn't that just mean there is a lot of competition?

No, it's less risky to go into an established niche or industry because it's already clear that there is money to be made, as people need and are already paying for that product or service. There are already potential customers. Do your research. If there are more buyers than providers or sellers, which is likely, then go and get some of those buyers. Start with your skills and interests, pick something that you can do or provide now.

You want to make sure you're earning a profit from your side hustle or else it's just a hobby that is costing you money not increasing your income. Remember the financial phases we discussed earlier. In the beginning you'll have more expenses than revenue. However, as you keep progressing you will earn and grow a profit.

Have a plan and a financial goal for that money when it's earned. By earmarking the money for a specific goal, you will help decrease the likelihood that it will be "wasted" so to speak.

Alright, now for the next lesson...

To reach success you have to have a plan. For some people, the plan is extremely detailed, while for others the plan is less fleshed out, but they still have one.

Your success is dependent on you actually utilizing and executing your plan. Consistently optimizing and following this plan is what will help you reach your goals and establish financial security.

Personal Finance Lesson 3: Budget is LIFE.

Yep, this one is about the B-word, BUDGET.

A budget is not just for when money is tight. A budget is not just for when you feel restricted or think you need to get spending under control. That's what most people think of when they think of a budget. You've probably heard people say things like "I can't. I'm on a budget." "I wish I could go, but I'm on a budget." "Oh no I can't do that, I'm on a budget."

You're ALWAYS on a budget. Sometimes you have to spend a lot of money on needs. Or it's a month or time of year where you have a lot of out of the ordinary expenses, so you don't have as much money available for wants or entertainment.

In such instances, that's when people bust out those phrases. What they're really saying is that money is tight and extra close attention is being paid to their budget. Many people also use those phrases if they don't truly have a budget and just know they don't have a lot of money left to spend.

If you're finding creating a budget to be hard, well ... there is a very good reason for this, budgeting is not just about the dollars and cents.

Money is important because of what it allows us to do and have. When trying to analyze your money, you're confronting what you're able to do versus what you want to do. It can be hard and emotional facing those numbers.

For example, as you try to determine how much you can save, you're thinking about all of the reasons why you need to or want to save. You're thinking about things that could affect you and your family, the good and the bad. You're thinking about past experiences, those you want to repeat, and those you never want to go through again. All of this comes up and plays in the back of your mind or is front and center.

Money is emotional because of all the baggage that surrounds it.

Money is just a tool. One that allows you to purchase and do things that you want or need to do. The projects or activities that you need this tool to complete bring on the emotion.

I get it. Take a deep breath, get centered, and do the budget anyway. Make it non-negotiable that it will get done no matter what. Your budget is going to help you have a healthy relationship with money aka this abundant tool.

A budget is crucial to your success. Everyone, irrespective of their wealth status, has a budget. You should not only have one too but be using it consistently. It is fluid and changes periodically as your life changes. As things come up or you are planning big life changes, you revise your budget and your money plan accordingly.

As you design your budget, recognize what may be coming up, good or bad emotions, and thoughts. Then use some tricks and tools to help you "do the budget anyway." Here are some things that may help.

1) Put your financial time on your calendar.
Set a CFO (chief financial officer) monthly meeting on your calendar. This way you will have carved out specific time to review your finances and your budget. This also helps couples to have a standing meeting where they can discuss their finances.

2) Create your budget in a calming space.

When it's time to do the budget, designate a space and put things that calm you into it. It doesn't have to be a large space or a separate room. If you do the budget at the kitchen table, then set up the kitchen. If you do the budget on the couch, then set up the room that couch is in or at least the space that you can see in front of the couch. Just set up the space.

3) Remind yourself that you have to design the plan to move from where you are to where you want to be.

This is an important reminder that it can take a while to reach your financial goals. Some goals can take months while others can take years to achieve. You have to make a plan and optimize it as necessary. The details of this plan may and very likely will change, but the goal does not.

4) Remind yourself that your financial security is important and worth some temporary discomfort.

Another important reminder. As you're working on financial goals and shifting behavior there will be some discomfort, it is unclear how long that discomfort will last. For example, paying off debt can take years, depending on how much debt you have. However, your financial security now and into the future is important, so to reach your goals you need to make it through this temporary discomfort.

5) Put some rules in place to help you stick to the budget and stay motivated.

It can be really hard to stick to a budget, especially during certain times of the year when special events come up, or after you've been using your budget for a few months.

Use tools and tricks to help you stick to your limits for your budget categories. Use a money calendar, or budgeting and financial tracking software to keep track of bills and incoming checks. A great trick to stay motivated is to use visual reminders.

6) Post your reminders and rules in the place where you design and analyze your budget.
Write down all the reminders that I have just mentioned and any that you come up with that help you stick to your budget and stay motivated. Post them prominently in that space where you're creating your budget.

They need to be visible. Out of sight is out of mind. Having reminders where you can see them, especially as you review your finances, will be very beneficial.

A budget has always been one of my key financial tools. If you aren't using a budget or haven't analyzed your budget, then I highly recommend you do so. For those with the Financial Planning Roadmap, don't skip that budget analysis section each month. You've got this, you can master your budget and your money. You want to be and become an entrepreneur who is not only bringing in a lot of money but also keeping a lot of it.

Beware of becoming a cautionary tale.

Remember these lessons resulted from implementing "go hard or go home" the wrong way. While the essence of this is true as you must push and give it your all, make sure you are giving your all to the right things. In my journey, I was unclear, or to be real – just confused and ignorant of what the right things were. Now you won't make the same mistake.

40

I learned that I needed to work smarter THEN work harder.

Have you ever heard the saying "measure twice and cut once?" This refers to the fact that you have to plan and then double-check before taking action. This is an important concept to adhere to for your business. If you go hard without a plan, you will waste a lot of time, energy, and money.

For every aspect of your business, make a plan, and make sure it fits into the overall plan or strategy. Certain aspects of your business require a lot more focus and more of your time and resources.

Keep your focus on revenue-generating activities and marketing. People can't buy something that they don't know exists. You should be consistently marketing your business and learning about your target audience. When you "go hard" on these activities you will see a return on investment in the form of more awareness, more leads, and more clients and/or customers.

Chapter 5: Your Network and Support Team

I bet you've heard the saying "your network is your net worth" numerous times. You probably took this to mean that the people you interact with influence how much you will earn. It's similar to the proverb or old saying, "birds of a feather flock together." I remember hearing this so many times growing up. It became a reminder to be careful of who you hang around regularly.

Well, the saying is true. Your business growth will be affected by those you surround yourself with, both in business and in general. There are three major components of your network that you need to have for success. Let's review all sides.

Mentorship
I wish I had realized the importance of business mentorship much sooner than I did. No matter how smart, educated, organized, and strategic you are, you can and should hire a mentor. Getting in-depth mentorship is crucial for your business success.

If you are just starting and cannot afford to hire a mentor, then continuously consume their free content until you can pay for their in-depth information and/or services.

At every stage of business, you will need mentors. A good mentor helps you avoid wasting a lot of time, energy, and money. Entrepreneurship is one of those things that requires some trial and error and testing of ideas. Mentors will help you to minimize the number of errors and help you to avoid mistakes that can cost a lot of money. They will help you know what to test and how to analyze the data from those tests. The business story laid out in that data tells you how to be successful. If you can read and translate the data, then you will know what action to take to increase your revenue.

It is not likely that one mentor will be able to provide everything you need forever. Work with the mentor you need to get you to your next level of success. For example, when you are launching a business you need a mentor who can explain and guide you through the beginning phases. You will need help with things such as picking a lucrative idea, learning how to fully monetize your idea, how to set up your business, the legal aspect of setting up a business, designing offers, etc.

Once you've already launched or have been operating for a while, you will need a mentor who can guide you through the next phase. This may include things like optimizing your brand, marketing strategy, operations system, financial system, sales strategy, etc. It could be the same mentor or you may need someone new.

As you search for a mentor, think about what stage of business you are in and who could help you navigate to the next stage, as most mentors and coaches have specialties. For example, if you are looking to grow the audience for your business then you would want a mentor who helps individuals design powerful marketing and advertising strategies.

If you're looking to increase your sales, then you want a mentor that can help you with your lead generation and sales process. If you're looking to move from six figures to seven figures, then you would want a mentor who helps entrepreneurs make that leap.

You can find mentors by listening to podcasts, reading books, attending conferences, searching on social media, etc. The information provided on these platforms showcase their expertise and help you to create a list of who you may want to hire as your mentor.

Support

Becoming a successful entrepreneur with zero support has to be near impossible. I do not know of an entrepreneur who has done this. You would be hard-pressed to find one because having a support network is crucial. Yes, your mentor is part of your support work; however, you also need others.

It's important to have people understand and support your entrepreneurial vision. This will come in the form of other entrepreneurs as well as people who simply believe in you and your vision or goal. These may or may not include family and friends. I've seen people be incredibly upset because their family and friends aren't buying their products or services. They may not be your target audience, or they cannot reconcile the person they used to know with the entrepreneur you have become. Whatever their reason it is okay.

Focus on creating a quality product or service and positioning your brand. You need to attract those who need what you are offering. Also, let's be honest. You can't rely on only family and friends because you would very quickly run out of leads and customers and your business can't scale or grow that way.

Support is not only monetary. There are other ways in which friends and family can support you in your business. They will and can share about you, your business, your products or services.

People love to share things that helped them, or that they think will help a friend or family member. Some will send encouraging or helpful information; these are huge supporters. I have friends who every time they see something about business or finance that they think will interest me or be useful, they send it to me. Great supporters will send information to help you develop and grow. Say thanks, apply what works for you and discard the rest.

Your support network is a great way to share and discover powerful resources for your business. Join entrepreneurial groups and masterminds so that you can be around like-minded individuals. These are powerful environments to gain insights and learn about resources that will help your business scale and grow.

Accountability partners are also an important part of your support team. This is a person or group that helps hold you accountable to achieving your tasks and goals. Remember earlier we talked about how sometimes you won't feel like working or completing tasks. Your accountability partners help you move through this to get the task done.

Sometimes simply knowing that you have to report your progress can motivate you to get those tough tasks done. I never want to be the one reporting, at multiple meetings, that I have to get the same task done or I haven't made any progress. On the flip side, knowing that you will be able to celebrate your progress and milestones with those accountability partners is very motivating.

Leads
Leads are another crucial part of your network for your business. You need to continuously be increasing awareness about your

business and what you offer. Without a flow of leads, there will be no customers, no positive cash flow, and the business will die.

You don't want to be the best-kept secret. When people say this, it is meant as a compliment. The great thing is that when people use your product or service, they love it, and that is why they make that statement: "you're the best-kept secret". It's like saying "how did I not know about this before" or "I wish I had known about this earlier." However, it also means that there is not enough awareness of your business and your offers. Only a few people know that you're there.

You want to maintain quality, as you break out of being the best-kept secret. Increasing marketing, advertising, and lead generation is crucial. You are letting people know why they may need you and how you would address their needs. In other words, show that you understand the problem or challenge that they have and that you have a solution.

Networking is the best way to naturally build your network and support team. Networking done right helps you to create organic relationships that are mutually beneficial. Networking is not only about finding leads and selling; it is interacting with like-minded individuals or potential customers. Make a list of events, groups, and platforms where you can interact with such individuals to completely build out your network and support team.

You have to be able to create a conversation. In-person events are the best in terms of getting this done. However, I have also developed strong relationships with people I met online by taking the conversation offline. Get on the phone or have an in-person meetup with that individual and have a real conversation.

Remember that networking is about creating mutually beneficial relationships.

Shiny Object Syndrome

Why You'll Never Leave Startup Phase

This is a business killer that is often not recognized, instead it is perceived as being innovative and productive.

Shiny object syndrome is when an entrepreneur constantly chases a new idea or hot trend instead of developing the current business.

We're going to discuss why some entrepreneurs never get out of the startup phase no matter how many businesses they start. Why this is happening and what it will take to stop it.

Why start a business?

Some of you are starting businesses and you'll never make it out of the startup phase. You'll never achieve that goal or satisfy the why that made you start on the entrepreneurship journey in the first place. You may be thinking "Hmm, what in the world is she getting at? What is she saying?"

Let me tell you why I made that statement, hopefully you can turn this around make your business a success and achieve your goal.

The factors that entice people to start a business vary. Some want to escape the corporate world which they find stifling and not an environment they want to work in forever or several decades. Some love the idea of creating their own schedules so that they can take better care of their families. Some, of course, want to be able to travel and experience new cultures and new adventures. Some know that entrepreneurship can be a key component to building wealth, and they desire not only to build their own wealth, but to establish a legacy of wealth.

Whatever the reason, many people are being enticed to start businesses. They are empowered, as we all are, by stories of those who have become successful high-earning entrepreneurs. They hear about the journeys and the progressions to earning five figures per month and six figures per month.

These stories lead to grand dreams of doing the same thing and achieving their goals. They imagine that amount of money coming in and the positive impact it would have on their dream lifestyles.

The Dream Goes Wrong

This is all great. I too love hearing stories about the rise to success, but that's not the problem. The problem comes later as you try to build your business. You jump into creating a business full force. You do research and you build. You do research and you build. Eventually you have a few sales coming in, but you're not even making enough to cover all your expenses. You're not yet breaking even.

You do more research. You hear of new techniques for marketing and sales. You learn more about them and you try them. You're still not making enough to cover all your expenses. You're still not breaking even. You're not making anywhere near what you would like or dreamed of making.

Then you hear about a new hot topic in business, or simply come up with a new idea that you're really excited about. You decide to focus on that instead. You do research and you build. You do research and you build.

Eventually you have a few sales coming in, but you're not even making enough to cover all your expenses. You're not breaking even. You keep trying new techniques for marketing and sales. However, you're still not making money anywhere near what you dreamed of making.

You're frustrated.

However, you still don' give up. You're determined to make this work. You hear about a new hot topic in business or simply come up with a new idea that you're excited about. You decide to focus on that instead. You do research and you build. You do research and you build.

Eventually you have a few sales coming in, but you're not even making enough to cover all your expenses. You're still not breaking even. You keep trying new techniques for marketing and sales but you're not making anywhere near what you would like or dreamed of making.

Again, you're frustrated. Then you get an idea for another great new business. Can you see what's happening here?

The Real Problem
You're putting in a lot of work and you're doing the research without getting the results that you want. You are thinking "What's the deal? What in the world is the issue?"

The problem is you're jumping ship too early. Before you've given the first business idea the time, energy, work, and money to make it a success you've already moved on to the next thing. The startup phase is NOT a certain length of time. It's not a certain number of weeks, months, or even years. Only once you reach certain milestones will you move out of the startup phase.

Some businesses don't break even for several years. It's several **years** of building their systems and an audience before they can get out their startup phase and see a real profit, and then increased profits. No, that's not everyone's story and it may not be yours but understand that you have to stick with your business to see the results that you want.

I'm not saying keep going with the same plan you made when you started the business as that definitely won't work either.

As you learn more (and you should always be learning more about your field and business in general) you revise and enhance your plan and your strategy to get better results. You then analyze these results and keep optimizing your plan to continuously improve the outcome.

You must continue to repeat that process. You can't do a few iterations of a plan then say; "okay this is a dud and I need to move on to this next thing because that's where the money is." If you chase the money, you will never catch it.

You've heard that there is no such thing as overnight success, but how does that show up? If you're starting a new business every couple of years, then this is you. If you're trying a new marketing or sales technique every month (or couple of months), then this is you. If you're constantly creating new products because the previous one wasn't selling well, then this is you. You're jumping to the next thing too early.

Go back to the entrepreneur success stories that you heard or read. Get the details and you will realize that each of those entrepreneurs did years of work and building before they reached success. Or they hired a top-notch mentor in the beginning that was able to connect them with the right people and help them work smarter. This then helped them cut down on the time it took them to make it out of startup phase.

I get that it is frustrating and there are times where you may say; "ugh why can't this just work." Believe me I get it and I wish I could say that goes away, but it doesn't. You'll keep making mistakes, but you'll learn from them and can then optimize and enhance your strategy accordingly. As you grow, you'll be working with more money and making fewer mistakes in certain areas.

How to know when to drop a business?
Now you may be thinking, "okay, but how do I know when I should shut down or keep working on my business?" The answer is to look at the data.

Calculate your gross profit margin. This will tell you if you're making a profit and how much. It is the percentage of your revenue that remains in the business after accounting for the expenses. When analyzing a specific revenue stream, it is the percent of revenue that remains after accounting for the costs of goods sold, which are the expenses that are directly tied to your product or service.

Take that into account when analyzing your gross profit margin. If your profit margin is negative (and yes, I've helped some clients calculate their gross margin and it was negative), then that means you are losing money. Your business can have an overall positive profit margin, but an individual revenue stream can have a negative profit margin. For that specific revenue stream, you are losing money with every sale.

This is why it is important to check the profit margin on each revenue stream AND the entire business.

How to survive the startup phase and how to get out?
We discussed the financial aspect of surviving to profitability. Let's look at a few other factors that affect your success in the earlier phases.

1) Stay at your job.
This is for the employed entrepreneur who is currently building their business on the side. If you have a job, then don't leave it unless absolutely necessary or if it is having a severe negative affect on your health. The paycheck can be used to handle the household bills and help build your business. Your job becomes your first silent investor.

This will lessen the stress as you build your business since you're not completely reliant on revenue or personal savings to survive. Remind yourself to be thankful that you're not in a scenario where you are stressed and desperate to figure it out as soon as possible to pay household bills like rent and food.

2) Have a learning schedule.
For each business system and piece of your strategy, learn more about it, and the tools you can use to better it.

Create a schedule of the topics so that you can strategically learn more and implement what you've learned to optimize your strategy and systems. Each time you optimize you should see a positive difference in your revenue.

3) Create a list of mentors.
Look at your learning schedule. Determine who are experts for each of those topics. Create a list of those experts so that you can learn from them.

Even if you don't have the money to hire them or purchase their courses, you can still consume their content and use any tips to move your business forward. Take encouragement from the entrepreneur realities they share, as no matter what their level of success, each entrepreneur continues to experience failure. You'll find that they don't let the temporary defeats stop them. You only fail if you stop trying.

4) Reinvest back into the business.
In the beginning, all the revenue you earn should be re-invested back into the business. This money can pay for your training (those business courses or that mentor's workshop), capacity building (buying the software and tools you need), and hiring assistance. Remember, it will get to a point where you cannot do everything yourself. Being able to hand off some tasks will free up time so that you can focus on revenue-generating activities.

Revising your plan for success.
As you learn and implement what you've learned, make sure you gather data on everything. You want to be able to determine how your actions are impacting your business and revenue.

To recap, these four items are going to be key in helping you get out of the startup phase.

1) Don't let yourself get entranced by the hot new trends or business ideas, as this may cause you to jump ship too early.

2) Stay at your job so that you don't have the stress of paying household bills as you build your business.

3) Keep learning about business and your industry. Take action on what you learn, since if you don't then there is no point.

4) As soon as you can, get a mentor. This will allow you to avoid many of the mistakes that will cause you to waste a lot of time and money.

5) Reinvest in your business until your revenue reaches a certain point where you can pay yourself.

Chapter 6: Combat Loneliness

Entrepreneurship can be a lonely road. Many people do not fully understand the ins and outs of building a successful business. There are so many struggles and failure moments experienced. There are so many milestones and successes that you accomplish.

These experiences shape, mold, and fortify you into a stronger version of yourself. However, they are experiences that you go through alone or with whomever you are building the business. It can be hard, nigh impossible, to fully convey the impact and importance of these experiences to someone who is not an entrepreneur.

We are social creatures, whether you are considered an introvert, ambivert, or extrovert. Our experiences create a foundation or glue for social interactions. When you are going through all of these powerful and life-altering experiences, somewhat alone, it can lead to a feeling of loneliness.

Many freelancers or solopreneurs may spend most of the day physically alone working on projects and tasks in the business. If you previously worked where you were part of a team, then you would have been interacting with coworkers throughout your day. Now as an entrepreneur just starting, or who has not yet built a team, you will be working alone for most of your day. Some entrepreneurs say that they can go days without seeing anyone. You can see how this too can lead to a feeling of loneliness.

What can you do to stay grounded and combat loneliness? Several things have worked well. The goal is to create meaningful experiences with family and friends and break up working alone. Figure out which combination works for you.

Schedule time with family and friends.

An entrepreneur's schedule is normally packed with business-related things. Make sure you block time on your schedule to hang out with family and friends. I know I'm preaching to the choir, but sometimes we get to the point where if it's not on the calendar it does not get done.

Be open to spontaneous meetups.

You can only have your nose to the grindstone for so long before you need to take a break to preserve your physical and mental health. I'm not saying to always be ready to drop everything and go, that's not practical. Be a little more flexible and willing to stop working and spontaneously hang out. with people, even if you *feel* like you should be working.

Do virtual co-working.

Consider doing virtual co-working sessions, as sometimes it's nice to have another person there. Each person works on their own business but stays logged into the same virtual meeting. It makes it easy to bounce ideas off each other or just to get the feeling that you are not working alone.

Use a co-working space or a café.

Offering co-working space is a trending business model, and there are many different options for renting or leasing a desk or office space. You could also work in a café that doesn't have a timeframe for you to leave. Purchase your beverage or meal and get your work done in a space with other people around you.

Schedule times to leave the house and do errands where you are among other people.

It can be easy to simply plug along doing work all day. However, if you're one of those people that will go days at a time without seeing anyone, scheduling time on your calendar to leave the house may be a good option. This will allow you to break up the day and interact with others.

Chapter 7: Business Failures and Lessons

Failure moments are your greatest lessons. As you progress on your entrepreneurship journey, you have had and will have numerous failure moments. Although at the time, it may not feel like it, they are a good thing. You're learning to optimize your business and serve your audience in the best way you can.

Here are some of my biggest lessons learned.

Not finding a job so I could bootstrap with a silent investor.
When I started my business, I stopped looking for a job and focused on building my business while living off of savings. There was so much to learn and implement and I spent a lot of money learning by trial and error. I also shot myself in the foot, so to speak, by not buying and investing in learning how to market and advertise. I was worried about money for pure survival and I had a very misguided idea about what it took to increase awareness and make sales.

Unless you have money saved in order to launch, operate, and run your household for a significant amount of time, keep your job. You can use part of your paycheck to invest in yourself and your business. Your job becomes a silent investor. This is a great way to look at it especially if you are in a job that you do not particularly like. I know it's easier said than done but it will be worth it.

Once you have replaced at minimum 80% of your salary with payments from your business, then you can move from being an employed entrepreneur to a full-time entrepreneur. This is money that you're able to pay yourself, not just gross revenue. The business should be able to fully operate and maintain its emergency fund AND pay you a salary. Once you have saved your money goal and your business revenue meets the aforementioned requirements, you increase your likelihood of success as a full-time entrepreneur.

Not consistently marketing.
With the use of social media and influencers marketing, it is a common belief of new entrepreneurs that social media will be enough. Social media is free and you see so many people have success by posting on these platforms.

Organically posting on social media is a great part of a marketing strategy and great way to start. However, it can take years to build up a large following, establish a brand, and establish that know, like, and trust factor. These three things are needed to bring in significant revenue, emphasis on the word significant.

Include marketing as part of your business budget. Your sales funnel can estimate the number of people you need to reach to achieve your target number of sales. Use a marketing estimator to determine how much money you will need for advertising to reach that number of people.

Not focusing on networking outside of my industry.
It's easy to network with others in your industry. It's a topic that you are passionate about and you may be attending the same events. Therefore, it's easy to have conversations and share resources.

However, I learned that it's important to also network with entrepreneurs in other fields. You'll learn other techniques and resources that you can apply to your business. Utilizing applicable methods from other fields and industries has allowed me to think outside the box and serve my audience better. In addition to industry-specific conferences and events, attend business development events and programs.

Affirmations and Epiphanies

We've gone through many business lessons, discussing ups and downs and how to get through them. I have explained the importance of affirmations.

I still use affirmations every day. They help keep me focused on my goals, and they silence the negativity monster and self-doubt that pops up every once in a while. They will help keep you positive, motivated, and focused.

The following section contains a set of affirmations. Pick one each day to reflect on and repeat. Whichever doubt you are having, pick an affirmation that addresses it. For example, there are times when you may think about your offer and wonder; "is this good enough?"

After doing your due diligence to make sure your solution or offer is the best that it can be, pick an affirmation that affirms the excellence of you and your products or services.

You've got this. You're an amazing entrepreneur who is getting better every day. Remind yourself of this.

I only create excellence.

My products and services are valuable and offer powerful solutions to my customers and clients.

I don't sell products and services. I provide solutions.

It's okay that they do not understand my journey. I will continue on my path.

Fear and doubt can accompany my actions, but they will not hinder my success.

Fear and doubt can be companions,
but I will not make them friends.

I try, I try, I try. I am tired YET I will try again.

I will speak about my business and tell others what I offer.

I will not keep my brilliance to myself.

I will focus 100% on my goals.

Failure is a part of success, but I will recover and keep going.

It's not easy, but it's worth it.

I will invest in myself, I am worth it.

I will make time for family and friends.

My health is a priority.

I will systemize my business for my success.

I will hire out for tasks that do not require my expertise.

I will try not to wear all the hats in my business. As I grow, I will hire help.

I've had a setback, but I will continue to search for other opportunities.

It's okay to pause, catch up, get myself together, and then get back to it.

I will plan for my success every day.

I will not give up. I may change the plan, but will not change my goals.

No matter the obstacles and setbacks, I will remain committed to my goals.

I will not make excuses. I will get results.

Quitting is NOT an option.

My solutions are needed by too many
for me to quit now.

I'm not only doing this for myself.

My why is greater than this setback.

Competition can't kill my dream, only I can.

I will not allow fear, doubt, negative self-talk, or inaction stop my dream from becoming a reality.

I will reach my goals.

I will make it to my desired financial freedom.

I will establish financial security.

I will have an overflow of abundance and prosperity.

I will build my wealth to where I desire it to be.

I will conquer this debt.

My revenue will continue to grow quarter by quarter, year by year.

I know having money, being rich, and being wealthy are separate situations.

I will grow my net worth.

I am the ultimate wealth builder and nothing will stand in my way.

Abundance flows to me.

I will take my time and build my business foundation properly.

I will review my financial data to make better decisions to grow my revenue.

I will regularly review my marketing and sales results to determine my return on investment.

I will invest in tools to efficiently use and maximize my time.

I will not be afraid to ask for assistance.

I will ask for assistance from experts in their fields.

Feelings of defeat will not lead to actual defeat, if I do not feed them.

Every day I will take actions that further my dreams.

I will not grow alone.

I will not settle for good enough.

I'm too great to settle for mediocrity.

Don't stop just because someone's bigger or been in the field longer.

No one can do it like me.

Success requires work and sacrifice.

I'm willing to sacrifice for my dream.

Create written agreements with every partner that all parties sign.

Surround yourself with people who support you, people who push you to be your best.

Recognize and appreciate each step in the journey.

Each failure holds a valuable lesson for your inevitable success.

Ask. If you don't ask, you can't get a yes.

I will strive every day to do better than I did yesterday.

I will continue to remain humble and appreciative.

I am worth the effort. I will keep going.

Their story isn't my story. I will keep working towards my goals.

You don't need the whole pie, just a slice. There are 7 billion people in the world. Help who you can.

Use whatever resources you have available and can afford to get the job done. As you grow you can gather more resources.

I am frustrated, but I will NOT quit. I will not give up.

I will create an action plan to achieve my goals.

Break up large goals into sub-goals for each quarter, then each month, then each day.

I will be a successful entrepreneur.

I am GREAT. I can do this. I will keep going.

Think outside the box.

If you're too comfortable you're not pushing yourself enough to turn your dreams into reality.

Every dollar has a job. Your budget has the jobs list.

What work am I putting in today to actualize my dreams?

It's not about what I want, it's about what my customers and clients need.

Survey your customers and clients to find out how you're impacting them and what else they want or need.

It's okay. Pause. Refocus. Regain
positivity. Now get back to working
the plan.

Congratulate yourself for what you're able to do now, even while focusing and planning for your goals.

You are smart, beautiful, and strong.

Keep motivating yourself. One dose won't last until you reach your goal. You need daily boosters.

You don't have to suffer to feel like you're doing everything you can for your dream.

I claim productivity and profits.

I will take at least 15 minutes every day to do something small that I enjoy.

Find a mentor who is doing what you desire to do and how you desire to do it.

When I feel "doubt" I will repeat to myself: I can do it. I will do it.

If I want new results, I will take new actions.

When overwhelmed, take a step back. Do a positive de-stress activity. Now, look at the plan and tweak it as necessary.

Before you toss out a plan make sure you have all the feedback and learned all the lessons.

Success is already mine. I'm on my way to get it.

Money has as much power as YOU give it.

You have the power to steer your day any way you choose.

Make it count.

Time is more valuable than money. No matter what you do you can't earn or get more time.

Review your business strategy often as it's the plan for your revenue.

Seek out new technology.

Sometimes, you're only as good as your tools.

Give it your all.

Tools, knowledge, and commitment turn dreams into reality.

I'm making a conscious decision to move past uncomfortable. Yes, it's nerve-wracking, but a needed step to reach my goals.

You are the chief financial officer of your finances and your household.

Make your own luck.

Preparation is key to success.

I will not succumb to fear.

What if it's not good enough?
What if it's exactly what they need?

Price is not the same as worth or value.

Don't lower your prices to match a customer and/or client's level of resources. Let them come back when they have the resources to invest with you.

You don't need to explain your worth.
Your actions, information, services,
and products do that for you.

Consistently and persistently invest in yourself.

Network often. Your network really is your net worth.

In person networking is best, but relationships can be formed over the phone and online. Just do it. Send a message.

Always be learning and increasing your skillset.

You are your biggest asset.

Just because it seemed like a good idea doesn't mean it actually is. That's okay. Just re-work the plan.

When I feel like a fraud, I'll remember, just because it comes easy to me doesn't mean it's not valuable to others.

I will keep my mind open to opportunities.

I will not allow negativity from anyone (even friends and family) to cause me to stray from my path.

Free will only take you so far.

In order to grow you will need to purchase better tools, information, and advice.

I will not cater to those that do not understand my journey.

Launch new products over a few months, don't just announce them.

Don't take it personally when people within your personal circle don't purchase or use your services.
Perhaps it's not for them.
Perhaps they don't understand your value.
It doesn't matter.

You never know where you'll have a conversation that may lead to an opportunity, so dress accordingly.

Your brand encompasses you as well as your products and services, customer relations, and the environment you create for customers and clients.

Chapter 8: Guidance, Mentorship, Community

We discussed key components to your success as an entrepreneur: knowledge, strategy, taking action, community, support, and accountability.

I would be remiss if I didn't tell you about my solution to offer all of those items: WISE Financial Fitness.

WISE Financial Fitness will help you master two essential skills for building wealth: making money AND managing money. They are separate skills and you need to cultivate both of them.

I know that as an entrepreneur, your business is your baby. You're working on keeping it growing and may sometimes neglect your personal finances in order to do it.

We've all had those times where we didn't pay a bill, not because we didn't have the money, but because we were so focused on business tasks.

I've coached and spoken with entrepreneurs who are so focused on growing revenue but don't pay much attention to personal finance. They just make sure everything was paid.

You can't build wealth that way and you'll sabotage being able to achieve and sustain your desired lifestyle.

You don't want to be an entrepreneur earning multiple six figures with close to zero dollars in saving. Yes, it happens.

I know if you're just getting started, you're thinking "well, let me make the money first." Make more money, but don't leave your personal house in shambles.

Remember your why for starting the business in the first place.

Money does not buy happiness, but financial stability and security surely bring peace of mind.

Having enough income to cover bills and maybe treat yourself is not enough. You deserve to be able to go on a vacation and remain prepared for an emergency.

You deserve to be able to help your aging parents and still be able to handle all bills and an emergency with ease.

You deserve to be able to give your family the best life and set your children up for future financial stability AND still be financially stable and secure.

One of the common goals that I hear has to do with financial stability for family members. To be able to not only set an excellent example for children but also to allow the creation of generational wealth, is the dream.

You deserve to achieve time and financial freedom. Whether you are using your business to achieve this or using income from a job, you don't have to struggle to do it alone.

That's why I tore apart and completely rebuilt WISE Financial Fitness to help you achieve time and financial freedom.

WISE Financial Fitness will help you:

- start and grow a business
- design systems to optimize your income
- budget like a boss
- save hundreds to thousands more dollars
- pay off debt and stay out of debt
- start building wealth

When you join WISE Financial Fitness, you'll have …

The skills, resources, and support to uncap your income, so you have more money to upgrade your lifestyle.

- Get that juicer and blender you've been drooling over.
- Hire that personal trainer you've been dreaming of working with to get you tight.
- Pay for the college tuition out of pocket with no worries.
- Pay for a new car with cash. Can we say no car note?!
- Upgrade your wardrobe with quality pieces with no guilt and using all cash.
- Afford your dream wedding with no financial stress.
- Prepare for a new baby the way you dream of doing.
- Eat at that upscale restaurant ordering whatever you want without critically eyeing the prices.
- Live your best life!

Personalized Guidance

You can get paired with a money scientist (business or finance consultant) who will help and build out key business systems or tools needed for success. It can be difficult to apply concepts to your unique situation. Your consultant is not only there to explain concepts but help you implement them. Your consultant will help you accelerate your revenue and journey to financial and time freedom.

Step-by-Step Curricula
Courses to upgrade your business and increase revenue. Some topics include:

- Picking your business idea
- Crafting your offers
- Determining Startup costs
- Determining your fees
- Pricing products and services
- Creating sales funnels
- Getting clients and customers
- Optimizing sales funnels
- Designing a financial system

Is not having an idea holding you back from starting a business? We can help you pick an idea and make sure it will be profitable.

Are you already in business, but need to increase revenue and profits? We can help you be able to spend more time working on the business than in the business. Don't create another job for yourself.

These courses will help you:

- Create long-term wealth
- Get consistent sales to increase revenue
- Escape the cubicle
- Build a business that can upgrade and support your lifestyle
- Remove the business finances confusion so you can take actions that increase revenue

- Be able to spend more of your day doing things you love and with people you love

Courses to keep and grow more of the money you make. Some personal finance topics include:
- successful budgeting
- saving acceleration strategies
- debt elimination methods
- key insurance types and why
- retirement preparation
- buying a home/car
- funding higher education

These courses will help you
- save money consistently faster
- be in complete control of your cash flow so that more money goes toward financial goals
- pay off your loans and become debt-free
- establish financial stability and financial security
- upgrade your lifestyle without money stress or guilt
- build long-term wealth and create a legacy of wealth

Resources for Higher Revenue & Better Money Management:
WISE Financial Fitness has templates, tools, and resources that will help you quickly get and stay in action. Some of the powerful resources include:
- Speaker Fee Pricing Tool
- Sales Estimation Worksheet
- Simple Business Budget Template
- Revenue Pyramid Template

191

- Sales Funnels Template
- Annual Budget Template

Go to https://wisefinancialfitness.com/brave to join with powerful bonuses.

BONUS:

Let's Network

We talked about the importance of networking. Well, I host virtual un-networking events that give you structured activities and time to showcase your expertise.

Here's your free ticket to the virtual un-networking event:
https://pocketofmoney.com/bravegift

Traditional networking events are usually inefficient, barely effective, and a bit tedious. Online, it's a similar process.

Let's evolve the process. There is a much better way to showcase yourself, learn about others, and establish mutually beneficial relationships.

Don't miss the next installment…

The Clever Entrepreneur's Desk: Right Revenue Streams and Business Models to Accelerate Profits

You need a winning strategy to successfully grow your business. Three crucial components are your business model, your revenue streams, and your pricing structure. Let's discuss how to design a powerful action plan for your business success.

Don't worry, we'll keep it just as real, fun, and down to earth. Stay tuned!

About Dr. Maria James

The short version ...

I founded Pocket of Money to help you take control of your money and live a world-class lifestyle. I am constantly studying finance and modifying the tools I create in order for them to be the most effective and useful. I want to empower you with the knowledge, tools, and skills you need keep more money in your pocket and build wealth.

I believe financial literacy is important and necessary to manage your cash flow. However, an important thing I learned from years of working with clients is that it's not just the knowledge but taking action on that knowledge day in and day out. Creating wealthy habits is key for financial success.

Fun Facts:
1. I, with my older siblings, started my first business when I was 10 years old. We sold juleps aka frozen cups.
2. In college, I learned to stretch the money I made during the summer over the entire 10-month school year.
3. I opened my first investment account at age 19.
4. In college, I co-founded a non-profit with my big sister and a friend: Heal a Woman to Heal a Nation, Inc.
5. In graduate school, I saved over $10,000 while on a stipend of $23,000 after taxes.
6. My PhD is in Cellular and Molecular Medicine from Johns Hopkins School of Medicine. Yep, I wore a white lab coat and did experiments.
7. I will never voluntarily pick a cold-weather vacation spot. Bring on the beach! It's the Caribbean in me.

The longer version …

I've always loved finance. I was born in St. Croix, US Virgin Islands and moved to Upstate New York at the age of five. I am one of nine siblings and a daughter to two awesome parents.

I learned a lot about managing money growing up in a large household and discovered my skill in organizing and finances. I opened an entrepreneurial business with my older brother and sister at the age of ten. We sold juleps (a frozen treat made from juice) for 25 cents a cup during the summer.

My parents were my first financial backers and made sure I learned important lessons from the experience. I had to calculate how much it costs to make one julep, determine my selling price, and then confirm if I was making any money. I had to tell them who was going to buy the juleps and what I would do with the money I earned. Important lessons!

We were making some good money until friends next door also thought it was a great idea to sell juleps and started selling theirs for ten cents a cup! We couldn't compete with those prices and shut the operation down after two summers, but the lessons about finance and business lasted forever.

I went to Wilson High School (let's go Wildcats!) and participated in the International Baccalaureate Program. During high school, if I wanted any extra clothes or shoes outside of what my parents provided, I was required to buy them myself. I then joined a program that provided work opportunities for students with good grades. I started working and opened my first savings account with $9 when I was 14 years old. I kept asking (I'm sure she would say bugging) my Mom to take me down to the bank and when she finally had a day off she did. I worked every summer of high school and stored the money in my savings account. It was during this time that I truly began noticing how I thought about money compared to how others thought about it. I raised $17,000 for college and I graduated as salutatorian of my high school class.

I then moved to Baltimore, MD to attend Johns Hopkins University, where I pursued my interests in Spanish, biology, and public health. I did a short study abroad, in Costa Rica, which was a great experience. I started to contemplate money on a global scale as I considered the monetary exchange rate, (which changed every day, in my favor) and how the pricing of various items differed in Costa Rica versus in the U.S. I was shocked at having to pay to use public restrooms near shops and restaurants, but could grasp why this was practiced.

During college, I greatly advanced my skills in personal finance. For the first two years I had to stretch the money I had made during the summer, to last the entire school year. Just think, I had to take my summer job earnings and make it last an entire ten months until I began working again. Some of the lessons I learned include being very strategic with cutting costs, tricks to stay disciplined with spending and saving, and using and developing money monitoring tools. During my junior and senior years of college, I began working part-time during the school year, by then I felt I had a handle on my studies and could work and study at the same time.

I then decided to pursue a graduate degree directly after college that would give me a stipend of about $27,000 per year. Those personal finance skills came in handy and were improved even more, especially with the addition of more monthly bills. While earning my PhD in Cellular and Molecular Medicine at Johns Hopkins University, I also honed my skills in analytical and critical thinking, and attention to detail, which I then also applied to finance management.

I continued to acquire skills managing money and personal finances on an extremely tight budget. Graduate school allowed me to further develop strategic planning and scientific analytical thinking and apply those methods to money management. The Money Scientist™ was born. On a stipend of $27,000 (about $23,000 after taxes), I saved over $10,000. I determined the science of managing money and building wealth. Applying scientific methodology to money allowed me to create a money strategy that elevated my lifestyle and grew a nonprofit.

I co-founded the non-profit organization Heal a Woman to Heal a Nation Inc. (HWHN). I was the Director of Finance at HWHN for ten years. While I was in college, we began empowering women in the community through a one-day conference. I assisted with the first HWHN conference in 2004. I was moved by the reaction of the women to the information provided and the experience of the day. I then became part of the conference planning committee for the subsequent nine years.

In 2008, HWHN, Inc became a federally recognized non-profit organization. Volunteering as the Director of Finance at a non-profit that serves hundreds of women a year has allowed me to enhance my skills in managing finances and overcoming financial obstacles, especially conducting public health programming on a sparse budget. I have volunteered at HWHN for so many years because of my belief in the mission and vision, as well as my desire to help women acquire the tools and knowledge to better themselves, their families, and their communities.

I founded Pocket of Money, LLC to share my knowledge of financial management and growth. I am constantly studying finance and business and modifying the tools I created in order to be the most effective and useful. I believe financial literacy is important and necessary to manage your cash flow and build wealth. I can help you to take control of your money and live a world-class lifestyle. I want to empower you with the knowledge, tools, and skills you need to control your money and live your best life.

www.ingramcontent.com/pod-product-compliance
Lightning Source LLC
Chambersburg PA
CBHW071602210326
41597CB00019B/3357